Think Your Way to a Better Marriage

A 30 DAY DEVOTIONAL

RELATIONSHIP LIFE COACH, CARNISA BERRY

SECOND EDITION

Think You Way to a Better Marriage

to a

RELATIONSHIP LIFE COACH, CARNISA BERRY

SECOND EDITION

ISBN-13: 978-0-692-02676-2

Cover design and book layout by Carnisa Berry

Edited by Cheesette Cowan

Dedication

I dedicate this book to my husband, Mr. Andre E. Berry for his continuous love, support, and commitment to the process of us "becoming one". Thank you for supporting my personal and spiritual growth and for encouraging me while I was writing this book.

I also dedicate this book to my children, DeMarcus, Bryson and Brianna. I love you all so much. I hope this book will one day bless your marriages.

Introduction

In a perfect world, you and your mate would walk down the aisle into a life of wedded bliss consumed by romantic dates, cozy night caps, and beautiful vacations to exotic destinations. However, the reality is marriage, albeit blissful, can be quite challenging at times. Contrary to the image portrayed by many Hollywood movies and love stories, it takes a lot of time, love and understanding for the "two to become one".

Successful marriages are the result of oneness in every area. The goal must be to become one in values, finances, and spirit. As simple as this may sound, achieving this "oneness" is a process that very few people understand. As a result, marriage can become hard, frustrating, and quite difficult—and let's be honest, most of us did not stand before God, our family, and our friends to commit to difficult. We married for unconditional love, to spend a lifetime with our "soul mate" and to live happily ever after, right? Then why do so many people struggle to stay married?

For many, the problem is that no one taught us how to operate in this wonderful, all-is-beautiful kind of love. Therefore, when hard times hit and misunderstandings surface, there's a tendency to think that we may have married the wrong person. Even worse, we believe something is wrong with us, our spouse, or our marriage; however, the truth is, the difficulties we face in marriage are all a part of "the two shall become one" process—They are not a reason to quit!

Whether you are a married veteran, newlywed, or single, I wrote this book both to encourage and empower you to succeed during the process. Your marriage can be good—even great; but, it's going to require your effort and commitment to God, each other, and the process.

Also, I wrote this book to help you understand that you are not alone. We all struggle in and during the process, but you don't have to give up. In fact, you cannot give up! Forge ahead because better days are just around the bend.

My prayer for you is that with each day of this devotional you are encouraged, your marriage is uplifted and your strength renewed.

I want to preface this book by saying I understand some readers may be in an abusive relationship. To those who are, I encourage you to get out of harm's way. Seek help and healing through a minister, counselor or life coach.

Ask yourself...

This book will help you have a new prespective on your marriage. Take time to began your new journey by answering these questions.

Wedding date: _____

What where your thoughts and beliefs about marriage and your spouse on the day you got married?

A: Scared but anticipated do what's to come.

F: I'll be like Jesus. I feel nervous, scared, excited, and stepping into servanthood.

What are your thoughts and beliefs now?

_____

_____

_____

_____

_____

_____

Day one

For this reason a man shall leave his father and his mother, and be joined to his wife; and they shall become one flesh.

— Genesis 2:24 (NIV)

Marriage is a Path to Wholeness

Marriage is a cocoon that allows us to grow and develop into our greater selves. It is where we learn to sacrifice, serve, forgive, grow, and most importantly, love without conditions.

God created marriage and everything God creates has purpose. There is a purpose for your marriage far greater than your happiness. God is concerned with your wholeness, and marriage is the vessel He uses to make wholeness a reality in your life.

The covenant of marriage is a lifelong promise we keep until death do us part. It is our greatest opportunity to die to self truly and eradicate the selfishness that is an enemy to our wholeness. The problem is most couples enter into marriage with selfish motives. They have an, "I have to be happy or else" mentality that leads them to believe it's their spouse's job to make them happy and satisfy all their needs; when in reality only God can do that.

Remember, God is a selfless God. Why would He create anything that promotes selfishness? We were created in His image and we are capable of His character, but we cannot become like Him in our marriage if we do not know Him and trust in Him alone to meet our needs.

The greatest gift you can give your spouse is surrendering your will to God's will. Doing so will open your heart to learning God's plan and purpose for your marriage.

If you are reading this book it is likely because your way has not produced the results you desire, so why not try God's way? I guarantee that doing it God's way will help you find all the happiness, love, joy and peace your heart desires!

3

Day two

All hard work brings a profit, but
mere talk leads only to proverty.
— Proverbs 14:23 (NIV)

Marriage requires hard work!

Marriage isn't easy by any means. In fact, most often it's hard work. However, it's a rewarding and fulfilling assignment that is well worth every sacrifice you will ever make. Marriage is worth holding your tongue when you are tempted to complain about your spouse to others. It's worth the effort it requires to speak to your spouse in love when every part of you wants to curse them out. It's worth your total devotion, and if couples would commit to doing the hard work, many marriages would reap the benefits of God's blessings on their unions.

The Proverb on the opposite page makes me very excited. I like that it says ALL hard work brings profit. One definition of profit is "benefit or gain". So, we can be encouraged by the fact that our labor as a husband or wife is never in vain. We can rest assured that God promises us a profit, benefits, and gain if we are willing to do the "hard work" during the tough times in our marriage.

Several years ago, my husband and I were faced with one of the toughest challenges in our marriage. The easiest thing we could have done was focus on the pain, hurt, and frustration of the situation, which in turn would have allowed us to remain full of rage and anger. Without a doubt, the emotions we felt were very real, and some might even say justified; however, we have learned that anger and rage never produce happiness or peace.

Andre (my husband) was brave enough to look inside of himself as he sought the root cause of his actions. It was during his time of reflection that he began to realize that his self-worth had been deeply wounded by the struggles of his past. At the same time, I too had to be willing to acknowledge my own shortcomings and discover what life lessons this experience was supposed to teach me. It was then that I began to understand that the pain of my past had taught me to believe that appearances were more important than actually dealing with the reality of situations. As a result, I had also become an unknowing, but willing participant in our unhappy marriage.

God desires for us to live a life of freedom. He wants us to be healed from our past pain and free to love unconditionally and without reservation; but although He's granted us healing, it's going to take some effort on our part to truly walk in it.

Our God is a Rewarder; and just as His Word promises in Proverbs, He will not be slow in rewarding hard work. Andre and I can testify to that. Today, our marriage is better than either of us believed was ever possible. We did the hard work, and our faithful Father gave us His reward. We both sought individual counseling to heal our personal pain; and doing so allowed us to reunite as two whole people, ultimately empowered to do the work necessary to heal our marriage.

Remember this Proverb also offers another promise—the promise of poverty: ... but mere talk leads only to poverty.

Talking alone will not yield favorable results.
Andre and I could have continued to argue, fight, and hold on to our pain, but what would that have done besides destroyed our marriage and delayed our healing. Furthermore, our lives without one another would have felt like poverty (deficiency and emptiness) to us both. So, I encourage you to be willing to do the work it takes

to restore your marriage and trust God to reward your efforts.

If you need to, seek your individual healing from your past pain, but at all costs go after the profit this Proverb promises. In the end, you and your spouse will be glad that you did!

Day three

Therefore each of you must put off falsehood and speak truthfully to your neighbor (spouse), for we are all members of one body. "In your anger do not sin": Do not let the sun go down while you are still angry, and do not give the devil a foothold.

– Ephesians 4:25 - 27 (NIV)

The truth about Anger

The real emotions behind anger are hurt, pain and fear. Unfortunately, it's easier to be angry than to feel the pain or fear that is associated with anger.

Anger takes the attention away from us. It allows us to look outward (as opposed to inward) and blame someone else, (for example, our spouses), for how THEY failed us. While this may make us feel empowered and give us a false sense of entitlement, it will never help us heal from our pain, nor will it restore our marriages.

Here are 3 ways that will help you deal with the hurt, pain and anger:

1. Face it! Do not focus on your spouse or the actions he or she did that may have caused your pain. Instead, connect to what you are feeling.

    I feel _____.
    A. Rejected
    B. Powerless, hopeless, or vulnerable
    C. Out of control
    D. Unworthy

2. Embrace it! If allowed, pain can reveal how your past is connected to your present. Use your pain to decipher how feelings from the past influence your current decisions and choices. More importantly, ask yourself, is there a pattern?

3. Erase it! Once you face and embrace it, then you are empowered to erase it! When you face your pain, you are connecting to the true source, as opposed to the person who triggered it. Once you are connected, you can begin to erase the pain by speaking truth to your feelings.

Here's an example of how I have used this method in my marriage:

When my husband was completing his Master's program, his routine was basically the same every day. He would get off work, eat an early dinner, take a nap, work on his online courses, and then he would go to bed. While I understood the importance of his time management routine, I missed spending time with him and wanted his attention.

Eventually, I began meditating on this thought: 'He never has time for me.' Soon, that thought sparked feelings of anger inside of me. I began complaining and became easily angered with him over the littlest things.

These arguments were senseless indeed. That's when I realized that I needed to connect to what I truly was feeling — I was feeling rejected.

Now that I had admitted that I was feeling rejected, I had to embrace those feelings. I had struggled with a fear of rejection for most of my life, so it didn't take much for me to welcome those familiar feelings back into my life. In times past, my fear of rejection caused me to create situations that would allow me to reject others before they rejected me. Needless to say, I did the same things in my marriage. I would start arguments with my husband and create more of the feelings of rejection I feared most. But I had learned that when we make decisions based on negative emotions, we create or give birth to what we fear, not what we truly desire.

The true source of my pain or fear of rejection was hurt I had experienced as a child. Cognizant of this truth, I had to look at my current situation objectively and not allow it to be shaped by negative emotions from my past.

The truth was Andre and I had agreed that if I needed some time with him, all I had to do was ask and he would create time in his schedule for me. We were both committed to him completing his master's program and we knew going in that it would require sacrifice. That is why we put these concepts and communication mechanisms in place to help us during this time.

So, why didn't I use them? Why didn't I just ask my husband to spend some time with me? The truth is, I was reacting and responding from my negative emotions instead of using the skills we both agreed to use when we began this process. I am just thankful that the three steps I outlined above helped me to get back on track and change my focus.

Remember, unresolved anger or pain will destroy your marriage, but you can experience freedom from your pain by accepting responsibility for your anger.

Day four

When you stop comparing what is right here and now with what you wish were, you can begin to enjoy what is.

— Cheri Huber

Stop Comparing

Stop comparing your marriage to someone else's marriage! No marriage is perfect; not even the ones where the couple appears to have everything you want. So, don't be fooled. Instead, focus on your spouse—focus on their strengths, as opposed to their weakness.

If you'll commit to this decision, you'll begin to see the greatness in your spouse, as well as the greatness in your marriage.

Day five

He that cannot forgive others breaks
the bridge over which he must pass
himself …

– Thomas Fuller

Forgiveness is for you

Deciding to forgive someone who hurt you can be challenging. Perhaps you struggle to forgive those who hurt you because of your belief about forgiveness. If you believe that forgiveness let's the perpetrator off the hook, then you are wrong. When you forgive, you remove the hook that connects you to your offender. When you hold on to un-forgiveness, its because you need someone to suffer for the pain you've experience. This effects your marriage because, if you aren't able to punish the correct person, you will punish the wrong person, and perhaps that's your spouse.

Choosing not to forgive will not protect your heart from being hurt again; it will, however, block your heart from giving and receiving all the love it's capable of. Forgiveness acts as an eraser in your life. It erases your connection to the person that hurt you and it removes the energy that attaches you to the pain of a hurtful experience.

Once your heart is clear from that pain, it's free to love. Remember, forgiveness will benefit you more than it benefits the people you forgive.

Day six

"'Love the Lord your God with all your heart and with all your soul and with all your mind.' This is the first and greatest commandment. And the second is like it: 'Love your neighbor as yourself.'"

– Matthew 22:36-40

A Command to Love

I've hear of people divorcing their spouse because they fell out of love. Love is much more than a feeling, it's a command. I want to point out that it wasn't Jesus' feelings that kept Him on the cross. It was love. If we view love as a feeling, it will be very easy to walk away from our marriages. When the feelings are gone, we tend to believe that the love is gone. However, true love is what shows up when the feelings are gone and the real work begins.

As it relates to love, it's time to get rid of the feeling mentality and embrace the commandment mentality. When you commit to this greater way of love, you can rest assured that any lost feelings will soon return.

When you believe your feelings for your spouse have gone, I advise you to love them with the type of love described in 1 Corinthians 13.

1. Be patient. Choose to be patient with your spouse and yourself during difficuilt times.

2. Be kind. Choose kindness even if you feel he/she does not deserve it.

3. Don't envy or boast. Resist the urge to envy other couples. Also, be sure not to boast if you find yourself doing more than your spouse as it relates to making your marriage work.

4. Show humility, not pride. Humble yourself

and ask for what you need. If you would like your spouse to help you with household chores, the children, or anything else, be willing to ask. Pride will cause you to be anger and upset with your spouse for not helping you, when you never expressed your needs.

5. Never dishonor your spouse. Do not use your with your words or actions to disrespect or hurt your spouse.

6. Be slow to anger. Anger is an expression of fear. Maybe you are afraid of losing your identity, power, connection, or love. Sort out what you are really feeling and then make a wise decision.

7. Don't hold a grudge. Learn to forgive quickly when your spouse offend you. Keeping account of their wrong doing will not help your marriage.

8. Speak truth. When you are hurting you will only see the worst in your spouse, speak truth about who they really are, not just who you perceive them to be during your anger.

9. Protect your spouse. Choose not to talk negatively about your spouse. Protect their character when given the opportunity.

10. Trust. When you can't trust your spouse, trust God to create the best outcome in any situation. Trust creates opportunities, distrust creates problems.

If you'll do these things the feelings for your spouse will soon return.

Day seven

A real decision is measured by the fact that you've taken a new action. If there's no action, you haven't truly decided.
— Tony Robbins

Make a Powerful Decision

We live in an age where some people do not prepare for marriage. The thought or attitude is, 'If marriage is too hard, I can always get a divorce.' When we make these types of decisions, we don't give our marriages a real opportunity to succeed. The power of our decisions are often under estimated.

If you decide that your spouse is the most beautiful person in the world, your decision will give birth to a power that will allow you to appreciate another's person's beauty without lusting for them.

You can decide that you will not seek affection, love, or attention outside of your marriage; and as a result of your decision, you will be prompted to seek wise counsel and pray if ever you find yourself feeling lonely, sad, or discouraged in the marriage. It's your decision that will harness the energy you need to avoid seeking fulfillment from someone other than your spouse.

You have to decide that your character is more important than your emotions and cast all of your insecurities and fears on God. Doing so will allow Him to restore you and preserve the best of you for your spouse.

It's all up to you! You have the power; now make the decision!

Week one

True growth require reflection!
Take time today and reflect on your
new thoughts about your marriage.

Day of Reflection

After reading week one, what new thoughts do you have about your marriage?

_____

_____

_____

_____

_____

_____

_____

_____

_____

_____

_____

_____

_____

_____

_____

_____

_____

Day eight

When you're surrounded by people who share a passionate commitment around a common purpose, anything is possible.

— Howard Schultz

Day of Reflection

Every marriage has a story. We all experience good and difficult times. However, it's usually the difficult times that shape the marriage. These experiences can make you better or bitter. Our struggles offer strength, determination, and compassion. They also offers anger, hatred, or discontentment. What you focus on will be the difference between living the happy life you desire or getting stuck in your misery of the experience. You can choose to embrace the sorrow it caused you or—the triumph it produced in you.

When you focus on the pain, its like building a wall, between you and your spouse. This wall becomes so big, you may believe there is no way around, over, or though it. But, that's not necessarily true. At any moment you can shift your focus to forgiveness and this will produce possibilities.

Possibilities remove obstacles. When you learn to concentrate on what's possible, its like using a ladder to get over the wall. Your ladder of possibilities will help you create your happily ever after story.

Here are 3 ways to create your new story:

1. Create a vision for your marriage.
Use a detailed list or vision board to get clear about the marriage you want. Begin focusing on all the possible things that can go right in your marriage, instead of what has gone wrong.

2. Take one action step towards the marriage you want daily.

Nothing happens over night. If you want to be happily married, the easiest first step you can take is, commit to the process. It will take work, determination, and focus, but you can do it. The effort it will take you to move toward your dream marriage is easier than the pain it's costing you not to.

3. Surround yourself with happily married couples.

I once read, we are the sum of the people we surround ourselves with. Are your group of friends a blessing to your marriage or a curse? The conversations you entertain will either help you grow or keep you stuck. The people you surround yourself with influence you more than you realize. In order to have your dream marriage, you will need happily married friends.

You only live once, I encourage you to live a happy fulfilled life. Your new story is just a thought away.

Day nine

You are your own worst enemy. If you can learn to stop expecting impossible perfection, in yourself and others, you may find the happiness that has always eluded you.

— Lisa Kleypas

Speak Your Expectations

One of the greatest things you can do for your marriage is to stop holding your spouse hostage to your expectations. Doing so puts both of you in bondage.

Rather than projecting your expectations on your spouse, try simply telling them what you need and allow them the right to accept or decide if they can or cannot meet that need.

Disappointments occur when we hold our spouse hostage to our expectations of them. We expect him/her to love or treat us a "certain" way, and we are disappointed when they don't measure up to a standard that they may not understand. We often do this to our friends, children, coworkers, and other relationships as well. We have our list of expectations and are inclined to think, 'I would be happier and my life would be better if people would do what I expect'. The reality is that it's illogical to demand others to rise to our expectations. Its even worse when we hold them to expectations we have not discussed with them.

More often than not, and without realizing it, we may be requiring something of our spouses that they are incapable of providing. It's important to understand that people can only give what they possess. For example, a person with a small love tank is incapable of filling yours. No matter how hard they try or how much they want to fill you, they simply cannot; and the relationship they have with you or the love they have for you will not change their capabilities. A broke man cannot give you money; and your expecting him to do so is illogical. Therefore, consider this: A broken-hearted person cannot provide you with love just because they are your spouse and you expect them to.

In marriage, we all must get to the place where we truly love ourselves. When we do that, we will understand that our spouses' lack or inability to love is not about us, even though it may affect us. The best gift you can give yourself and your spouse is to speak your need and express your expectations. Nevertheless, you must also be willing to accept that your spouse is not mandated to meet that need or expectation, or that they may be incapable of meeting it.

Today, make a pledge to set yourself and your spouse free from the bondage of your expectations. As you read day nine's devotional, consider that all humans have six basic needs, and these needs drive everything we do. In your personal time of reflection, consider all six and identify your two dominant needs. Once you understand what needs drive you most, you can speak to your spouse based on your needs and not your emotions.

1. **Significance** – the need to feel important and significant
2. **Safety** – the need to feel emotionally and physically safe
3. **Love and Connection** – the need to feel connected to some thing larger than yourself and to be loved
4. **Variety** – the need for change and stimulation

5. **Growth** – the need for spirituality and spiritual growth

6. **Contribution** – the need to give

Understand that expectations communicates a demand, however, express needs create opportunites.

Day ten

Mankind's greatest gift, also its greatest
curse, is that we have free choice.
We can make our choices built from
love or from fear.

— Elisabeth Kubler-Ros

Choose Healing

Every person that comes into your live is there to teach you something about you. This is why many of your best life lessons are often birthed from your most painful experiences. Knowing this, you have to look at every situation in your marriage as an opportunity for learning and growth. For example, when you are hurt by something your spouse has said or done, instead of looking at the situation and trying to find fault, look for the teachable moment and ask yourself, what can this experience teach me about myself?

I was in a situation recently that helped me discover that I am addicted to approval. It wasn't until the pain showed up that I was forced to examine my own behavior patterns, which led me to this understanding about myself.

We bring everything we are to our marriage—the good, the bad, and the ugly—and the marriage suffers because of the individual and internal pain we bring into it. Therefore, it's important that we make it a practice to self-evaluate.

Truth is, we can't heal from what we don't acknowledge. The first step toward healing is awareness. Once you are aware of the true source of your pain, you can choose to:

1. Blame your spouse and focus all your attention on them.
2. Ignore it and pretend it doesn't exist.
3. Connect to the root cause of it and seek healing.

The choice is yours!

Day eleven

The reason a lot of people do not recognize opportunity is because it usually goes around wearing overalls looking like hard work.
                    — Thomas A. Edison

Every Day is an Opportunity

Every day of your marriage is an opportunity to create a beautiful life. Are you making the most of your days, or are you letting your false beliefs and fantasies about marriage keep you from enjoying the rewards that come from doing the hard work required to maintain a healthy marriage?

Remember fairy tales are for books and movies. In the real world, anything worth having requires work; do the work and create beautiful opportunities in your marriage every day.

Day twelve

When a couple agrees about money, they agree about life. The flow of money represents the values under which your family operates. When you agree on your value system, you will reach UNITY in your marriage.

— Dave Ramsey

Wisdom and Money

It took me and my husband years of blood, sweat, and tears to get to the level of unity Dave Ramsey describes. Neither of us grew up with a systematic way of thinking about or handling money. Consequently, we both had varying views on the subject.

Money meant security to me, but to Andre it meant freedom. When we got money, he wanted to spend it, and I wanted to save it. As a result, we spent years disagreeing and arguing about it. It was the hot-button issue in our marriage—one we couldn't discuss without an argument. Eventually, we just stopped talking about it. We thought it best to leave the subject alone for the sake of avoiding an argument; however, we still did not have a solution or resolution where our finances were concerned.

For us, and most couples, finances are one of the last areas to come together in a marriage. It was only after Andre and I began healing the other areas of our marriage and recognizing our fears and needs that we were even able to tackle the area of money. In the beginning, neither of us had a plan or method for money. However, with God's wisdom we enrolled in Dave Ramsey's online program Financial Peace University which helped us develop a system for managing our finances. We now have an emergency fund, we have paid off most of our debt and we are saving money. We also have a plan for our retirement and our children's college funds.

I encourage you and your spouse to come together and pray for godly wisdom where your finances are concerned. Resist the temptation to trust in yourself knowing that there is a greater way.

It was wisdom that helped Andre and me get to a point where we could discuss money without an argument; and as a result, we enjoy a greater level of peace. This same wisdom is available to you, if you will only ask!

Day thirteen

To the victor belong the responsibilities.
— Al Bernstein

Be the Victor or the Victim!

Most people want to believe that their spouses should never do anything to hurt them; but the reality is that since our spouses are human, there will be times when they fall short of their best. There may be times when they fail to communicate properly, fail to disclose critical information, or worse. Yet in all of that, we have to decide whether we are going to be the victim or the victor.

Remember, you are the only person you can change in any situation. You don't have control over anyone else's actions; and when you exercise control over yourself, you are the victor because you are taking responsibility for what you have authority over. However, when you focus on your spouse—trying to change them—you are essentially powerless and have become the victim, thus relinquishing your responsibilities and your stake in victory.

When you blame your spouse for all your misfortune, you make yourself a victim, and ultimately powerless. If you blame your spouse for all of your pain, anger or disappointment, you then make them responsible for your recovery, healing, and joy.

However, you are responsible for your healing and recovery. You own your wholeness, not your spouse. Stop telling the story where everyone has power, but you. Take hold of your power. Become the star of your own life. Be the hero in your marriage. Stop reacting and become proactive. It's your life, and it's your marriage. Forget what your spouse is or is not doing, and take responsibility for your part in making your marriage great. That's what victors do!

Day fourteen

For God hath not given us the spirit of fear; but of power, and of love, and of a sound mind.

– 2 Timothy 1:7

Overcome Your Fears

Recently, I read an amazing book titled *The DNA of Relationships* by Dr. Gary Smalley. In the book, Dr. Smalley teaches different ways fear shows up in our relationships, especially our marriages. He explains that we all have what he calls, "fear buttons" and once these buttons are pushed, we enter into what he calls the "fear dance".

Fear buttons are our core fears. If you can't identify your core fear or how you react when your fear button is pushed, your marriage will suffer.

Core fears are feelings of: powerless, rejection, failure, unloved, abandonment, disconnection, helpless, controlled, etc. Once you are able to identify your core fear, you are empowered to respond to your spouse instead of reacting. Otherwise, you will continue to be a victim to your fear. Thus, continually creating the fear dance.

First, I encourage you to get the book, its an excellent read. Secondly, identify your core fear, so that you can gain victory over this area in your life. Lastly, help you spouse understand his/her core fear, thus creating a stronger relationship. We all have choices to make in life. And we can only make wise, intelligent, life affirming choices when fear is not the driving emotion.

The four major fears that typically control our behaviors are:

1. **Fear of rejection**
2. **Fear of losing of control (powerlessness)**
3. **Fear of being unworthy**
4. **Fear of failure**

Take time to learn your greatest fear. It's important to be vulnerable with yourself and your spouse. When you are willing to be vulnerable, you can identify your fears, confront them, and gain power over them. When you walk in your power instead of your fear, you can help heal your marriage.

Week two

Your thoughts are creating your decisions, and your decisions are creating your destiny.

– Carnisa Berry

Day of Reflection

After reading week two, are your new thoughts help you create a healthy marriage?

_____

_____

_____

_____

_____

_____

_____

_____

_____

_____

_____

_____

_____

_____

_____

_____

Day fifteen

I used to think I had marriage issues, however I begin to realize I had "me" issues. The more I worked on my "me" issues, the more my marriage issues begin to dissolve.

— Carnisa Berry

"Me" Issues or Marriage Issues

When my husband and I were first married, I was convinced that I made better decisions than he did. I believed that if Andre would just listen to me and do things my way, our marriage would be perfect. This way of thinking created lots of pain, hurt, and frustration in our relationship. I remember praying, asking God, "Please change Andre, fix him Lord!" God's response to me was, "What about YOU?" This response shook me to my core. At that very moment, I decided prayer time was over.

God's desire is to have a life altering relationship with each of us. He wanted me to acknowledge my issues, not Andre's.

Once I began to focus on my own issues, instead of Andre's, our marriage began to change. I began to realize that my discontentment with myself and my marriage, was because I was so busy comparing my life to everyone else's. Therefore, I couldn't appreciate what we had, because I was focusing on what we didn't have. I didn't know or understand my gifts, talents, or purpose, so consequently, I targeted Andre's short coming to avoid dealing with my own. These were just some of my "me" issues God wanted to talk about that day I was asking Him to fix Andre.

If you find that everyone in your life is causing you frustration, aggravation, and disappointment, perhaps God is inviting you to bring your issues to Him. It's easy to look outward and blame everyone for your problems and issues, however this will never cause your life to become better. I promise you, when you begin to do the "me" work, your relationship issues will get better.

Day sixteen

When we avoid God, when we are in pain, we avoid our healing.

— Jimmy Evans

The Path to Healing

Its obvious, that we all experience pain in our life. The worst thing about pain is not the pain itself, but the message behind the pain. Whether or not we are cognizant of it, all pain carries a message. A few examples of those messages are: I am not good enough, God doesn't care, everyone is against me, no one really loves me, I am worthless, etc. When these thoughts perpetrate your mind, you begin to live them outwardly. Once you have a deep belief that you are not worthy or that everyone is against you, you will produce behaviors that will cause you to create these experiences in your life. These messages will cause you to doubt your spouse's intentions and cause you to sabotage relationships.

There is another option. You can cast our painful burdens on God. When we do not seek God's healing for our pain, we will find alternative coping methods.

Here are the 4 common ways people cope:
1. **Medicate**: Use food, alcohol, sex, drugs, shopping, etc. to avoid the pain
2. **Motivate**: Keep busy to avoid the pain
3. **Meditate**: Focus on everything that's wrong in our life
4. **Denial**: Pretend the pain doesn't exist

Ultimately, it is God, not our spouses, who is responsible for our healing. Knowing this, we must always aim to take the broken pieces of our hearts and put them in the capable hands of a loving God. He loves us and will show us the path to healing and love again.

Day seventeen

The wise woman builds her house, but with her own hands the foolish one tears hers down.

— Proverbs 14:1

Choose Your Words Wisely

Your words contain power therefore, choose and use them wisely. Wives, it is with your words that you tear down your house (husband and family). Skillfully choose words that build your husband up, not tear him down. Remember, it's the power of your words that will either help create the marriage you desire or destroy it. When you are tempted to berate your husband, remember that no man has ever become great because he was insulted enough to change. Men were designed by God to desire and respond to praise. When you speak praise-filled words of adoration and respect to your husband, you ignite a passion in him that will propel him to become the man God created him to be.

Husbands, learn your wives love language. Learn to speak her language of love. It maybe words of affirmation, quality time, giving her gives, acts of service, or non-sexual touch. Once you learn to speak her language, you can open a door inside of her that leads to more passion and connection.

You marriage is only as strong as the words you speak to one another.

Day eighteen

Love brings you face to face with yourself. It's impossible to love others if you
don't love yourself.

— John Pierrkos

Love Yourself First

"… Love your neighbor as yourself …." –Mark 12:31 (NIV)

I wonder how married people would respond if this scripture read, Love your spouse as you love yourself.

Many would argue that they do love their spouses as they love themselves; and I would have to agree with their sentiments. With that being said, the real question becomes, do you even love yourself to the degree that you should?

If you don't love yourself properly, it will be impossible for you to really love anyone else, especially your spouse. If you are constantly judging yourself, deceiving yourself, and betraying yourself, you will do the same thing to your spouse.

Here's a thought: When you make promises to yourself that you do not keep, you are lying to yourself. When you lower your standard or compromise your morals to get what you want, when you want it, you are betraying and deceiving yourself. When you compare yourself to others or believe you don't measure up, you are judging yourself. And if this is the way you "love" you, this will be the way you "love" others. This is why all your relationships, especially your relationship with your spouse, must be predicated on your relationship with God. When you realize how much God loves you, you can allow His love to guide you into loving other people.

The best relationship you'll ever have is a relationship with God. Once you begin to understand how much He loves you, and you receive that love, you will begin to love and truly accept yourself; and only then can you love and accept your spouse.

If you are having a hard time loving your spouse, look within and spend time basking in God's love. Connect to loving yourself. It's almost certain that you will see your spouse in a different light after you emerge from God's presence.

Day nineteen

The wife does not have authority over her own body but yields it to her husband. In the same way, the husband does not have authority over his own body but yields it to his wife. Do not deprive each other except perhaps by mutual consent and for a time, so that you may devote yourselves to prayer. Then come together again so that Satan will not tempt you because of your lack of self-control.

— I Corinthians 7:4-5

Intimacy is Important

A sexual relationship requires consent. We give ourselves to each other. Because of this, sex is a sacrificial act between a husband and wife. It depends upon a serving spirit, which means the best sex in marriage is one person serving the other. That attitude is the secret of success within marriage.

Nothing else can guarantee sexual fulfillment. For instance, sexual chemistry will come and go. There will be physically good times and physically bad times. Hormones surge and sex may be great. But then we enter a stressful season of life and the sex takes a back seat to everything else.

You can't count on chemistry, but you can count on commitment. If I am committed to serving my wife every day of my life, then hormones or stress don't matter. What matters is that my spouse needs it, and I love her, and I have chosen to serve her.

Serving your spouse doesn't mean setting yourself up for abuse. It doesn't diminish the equality of your marriage. It doesn't mean you always have to agree, either. It just means you are choosing to meet each other's needs and desires.

Within marriage, servanthood is the only spirit that experiences true emotional, spiritual, or sexual intimacy. You simply can't be intimate with a selfish person.

God created sex and God loves it. He loves to see his people enjoying the special gift He created. He wants us to be adventurous and enjoy sex in many different ways—not sinful ways, but in ways that give each other pleasure.

Excerpt of an article by Pastor Jimmy Evan of Marriage Today Ministry

Day twenty

We see the world not as it is, but as we are—or as we are conditioned to see it.
— Stephen R. Covey

Is it true or just your Perception

Image from ocdqblog.com

This image is often used to teach a powerful lesson about perception and how it impacts our lives. If you focus on the picture on the left, you may perceive that the lady in the center picture is young and attractive. However, if you focus on the picture on the right, you may see the lady in the center as old and weary.

Our perceptions of our spouse and experiences are often like this example. What we focus on is what we see. This is how you and your spouse can have two totally different opinions about a shared experience. And it doesn't mean either of you are right or wrong, it's just your perception of a thing that differs.

We believe we see things as they are—we believe we are objective; however, most of the time, this is not true. We see the world not as it is, but as we are— or as we are conditioned to see it. For example, if you have been hurt, especially by your spouse, you may view the world and your marriage, not as it is, but—through the eyes of your pain. This can have a tremendous impact on your marriage because ultimately, it will make it easy for you to see the worst in him or her. As a result, you literally will hold them captive to who they were when they hurt you.

Consequently, you may begin to believe that your spouse can't change or won't grow. The most dangerous effect of negative perceptions is it robs us of hope. The reality is people can change; your spouse can change! And when he or she does, you must be willing to clear your perception of them, as well as, change your behavior toward them.

Day twenty-one

The safest principle through life, instead of reforming others, is to set about perfecting yourself.

— B. R. Haydon

Life is Offering you a Lesson

If you happen to think that all the arguments and disappointments in your marriage, are your spouse's fault, you are missing out on your opportunity to heal, grow and become a better you.

Situations show up in your life to teach you something about you, not your spouse. If you are constantly focusing on your spouse's behavior and not seeking ways to be better yourself, you are missing the lessons. What's worse is, if you continue to miss the lessons by refusing to deal with your own issues, you can expect the same situations to continuously occur.

Remember, the goal is for you to learn a lesson about yourself and for you to be better today than you were yesterday. In every situation, focus on learning a valuable lesson about yourself and let your spouse go through their own process of learning.

"Every man has in himself a continent of undiscovered character. Happy is he who acts as the Columbus to his own soul."

–Sir J. Stephen

Week three

Change only occurs in your marriage
when you change!

— Carnisa Berry

Day of Reflection

Are you there any changes in your marriage since you
begin reading this book?

_____

_____

_____

_____

_____

_____

_____

_____

_____

_____

_____

_____

_____

_____

_____

_____

Day twenty-two

He that trusteth in his own heart is a fool: but who so walketh wisely, he shall be delivered.

— Proverbs 28:26

Seek Wisdom

Financial freedom is a heart's desire for me—it is something I have been praying about for a long time. As I stated before, with God's help we were able to knock out our debt, but I didn't know how to acquire wealth, so that became my new prayer. When I first began to seek the Lord on this matter, He placed the scripture on the opposite page on my heart and that is what I began to pray. God's Word also tells me that when I knock, the door shall be opened, and when I seek, I will find. So, I sought the Lord for wisdom in this area.

That's when I began to understand it's not enough to pray for wisdom, but it's equally as important to realize that we must do our part in seeking it out if we truly aim to live above the things that hinder us from having God's best.

After some time passed, I came across and ordered Dave Ramsey's Financial Peace University course. I was determined that my tomorrow would not look like my today, and I expected things to be better on the other side because this Proverb tells me that whoever walks (stay in, moves in, and applies) wisdom will be delivered. Therefore, I expected nothing less; and neither should you if you have an area in which you want deliverance.

If there is an area in your life where you keep falling short, whether its concerning your marriage, relationships, parenting, emotional maturity, finances, or whatever, I encourage you to seek wisdom, walk in it, and be delivered.

Day twenty-three

The wicked commit slow suicide; they waste their lives hating the good. God pays for each slave's freedom; no one who runs to him loses out.
— Psalm 34: 21-22 (The Message)

Nothing is Ever a Waste

Understand that God does not waste anything, He desires to use everything to His Glory. So, stop wasting the gifts God gave you.

Stop wasting His grace by living your will and not His. God does not offer you bad ideas, anything He tells you to do or not to do, it is for your benefit not your detriment. He will give you the strengthen and grace to endure. For the husbands, you are told to sacrifice for your wife. Obey God and trust Him to provide you the wisdom and strength to give up whatever He is asking you to give up for the betterment of your marriage. Wives, you are told to submit to your husbands. Therefore, you must also, obey God so, your marriage can receive the benefits that comes with obedience.

Stop wasting your marriage by comparing it to other marriages. Don't focus on only getting your needs met, refusing to serve your spouse, instead be grateful for him/her. Marriage is not easy, it takes work for two people to become one in mindset, Spirit, and values. DO THE WORK! Love your spouse when you don't feel like it, speak kind words to each other, make your marriage about God and not about you.

Stop wasting God's joy, by being selfish. When you refuse to share God's grace, enjoy His mercy and live in forgiveness, you waste His joy. God blesses you every day with something to be thankful for so, if you don't think you have any reason to be joyful, you are focusing on the wrong things. Shift your focus.

Finally, stop wasting your pain, by wallowing in self pity, by being angry all the time or just being downright mean. It's unproductive; especially once you realize pain shows up to draw you closer to Him, so that He can help you heal from the pain. When you refused to step into your pain and use it to grow, you are wasting it. However, it will be back, because as I stated, God does not waste anything. He recycles.

Day twenty-four

Not that I speak in regard to need, for I have learned in whatever state I am, to be content: I know how to be abased, and I know how to abound. Everywhere and in all things I have learned both to be full and to be hungry, both to abound and to suffer need. I can do all things through Christ who strengthens me.
— Philippians 4:11-13 (NKJV)

Is your view Clear?

Have you ever worn tinted sunglasses? The ones with blue or red color lenses? If you have, you know that they distort everything you view, making everything look either blue or red. Well, that's how our internal belief systems work in our lives and in our marriages.

All my life, I struggled with a negative internal belief that said, I'm not enough. This deep fear tinted everything and everyone I encountered. I measured my husband, my home, and our lifestyle through the painful lens of "not enough." Adding insult to injury, I constantly compared myself, our marriage and my life to everyone and everything and they never seemed to measure up—they were always "not enough."

One day, I was listening to a sermon in my car when I heard the minister say that the apostle Paul knew how to be content in all things and in every situation. I immediately wondered, how did Paul learn to be content? The scripture the minister referenced was Philippians 4:11—13, and when I got home, I began to study this scripture and prayed for the same contentment Paul had.

Over time God blessed me with His peace, and I found it to be the only thing in life that I never wanted to live without. It was that peace that brought me clarity and contentment, and changed my outlook on life. Even my prayer life began to change when I was praying from a place of contentment versus a place of always wanting and needing more.

Ask yourself, 'Through what filter am I viewing the world and how is it affecting my life and my marriage?" "Am I allowing fear to be the lens through which I view life, or am I truly seeing life clearly?"

I realize now that my lens on life was all wrong. I know that I'm more than enough, just the way I am, through Christ. I see life differently, and as a result, I don't have to compare myself to others.

I look back over pictures from my past and now realize that I've been blessed with a beautiful life, a wonderful husband, and beautiful homes. I am surrounded by wonderful people who love me and whom I love; however, in times past, the tint on my lenses stopped me from seeing that, yet alone appreciate it. I thank God that my vision is clear now and I am a better person because of it.

Ask God to reveal the tint that might be affecting your marriage.

Day twenty-five

What we think determines what happens to us, so if we want to change our lives, we need to stretch our minds.

—Wayne Dyer

Remodel Your Thoughts

Trying to create a new look in a room using the same old furniture and artwork is only readjusting your existing look. To remodel or to create a new look, you must add new items. The same is true for your marriage.

Trying to create a new marriage with the old thoughts and behavior patterns is a futile undertaking at best. You may rearrange a few things, but there won't be any lasting change.

Just as remodeling a room requires new items to complete the transition, your mind need new thoughts and new behavior patterns to create a new marriage. If your current thoughts aren't producing the marriage you desire, it's time to remodel your mind with new thoughts—thoughts that are capable of producing new behaviors that will help you create the life and marriage you desire.

Day twenty-six

We can have no progress without change …

— John Wooden

Embrace Change

Change is a perquisite for growth in any area. Therefore, if you want your marriage to grow and be better, you must be willing to change.

Change is a spiritual process because our soul (thoughts, will, and emotions) is connected to our belief—who we are at the core—which is a spiritual being. With that in mind, in order to create an atmosphere for change, we must be willing to question and challenge the validity and soundness of our current thoughts and beliefs. We have to be courageous enough to be willing to admit that what we believe could be wrong. We need to be equally as courageous to accept that our new thoughts and beliefs oppose everything we have been taught by those we love and those who love us.

In the end, change requires our will to be linked with our new thoughts and beliefs. It requires us to control our emotions as opposed to being controlled by them.

Admittedly, change can be difficult, but it's not impossible; however, it is a prerequisite for living life on a greater level. And to create effective and positive change in your marriage, this is what will be required of you. The good news is you do not have to do this alone. God is willing and able to help you make the change.

As it relates to change in your marriage, answering the following questions will help you to create the open, honest environment necessary to experience the lasting change you desire:

1. Do you have positive examples of marriage in your family?

2. What is your honest belief about marriage?

3. Has this belief helped you or hindered you?

4. What is this belief based on—experience, examples, or ideologies?

5. Is it possible that there is a purpose for marriage greater than your belief about marriage?

Day twenty-seven

"Some of the biggest challenges in relationships come from the fact that most people enter a relationship in order to get something: they're trying to find someone who's going to make them feel good. In reality, the only way a relationship will last is if you see your relationship as a place that you go to give, and not a place that you go to take."

—Tony Robbins

Healthy Relationships

Unfortunately, many of us did not grow up with positive examples of marriage. We also did not grow up seeing healthy examples of male–female relationships. As a result, we must be deliberate about assessing and evaluating our views and beliefs about marriage and relationships. We must be willing to consider that our views might be misguided, self-centered, and even worse, destructive.

I encourage you today to be intentional about the health of your marriage relationship. Healthy relationships create an atmosphere for joy, respect, responsibility, security, integrity, strength, and growth. We have to be willing to regularly assess whether our relationship reflects these traits for us and our spouses, or whether we are just in the relationship to get our needs met.

Day twenty-eight

...And they lived happily ever after

Recognize Your Power

Let me encourage you by saying, your marriage can recover from whatever past hurts and pains you have experienced, if you and your spouse are willing to do the work it takes to get to a better place. Within you lies the power to create your "happily ever after," and that begins with evaluating your current beliefs, and if necessary, creating new ones to replace the old ones that have created your pain.

Consider this: Our thoughts, which are reflected in our words, only have the power we give them. The problem occurs when we allow our thoughts to blindly create patterns in our life that we don't connect to our conscious mind. It's almost like we're walking around in a zombie-like state, moving as if we have no power over our own lives.

It's imperative that we become cognizant of our thoughts if we are to make our marriage and life better.

Take a day to examine the thoughts that run through your mind and ask yourself:

1. How do these thoughts make me feel about myself?
2. How do they influence how I treat myself?
3. How do they influence how I treat others?
4. Do these thoughts make me feel empowered or powerless?
5. Do these thoughts make me a better person?
6. Are these thoughts helping me become the person I want to be?

If the answers to these questions are not the answers you want, know that this may be why you have not achieved your "happily ever after."

Day twenty-nine

For I know the plans I have for you, de-
clares the LORD, plans to prosper you
and not to harm you, plans to give you
hope and a future.

                        – Jeremiah 29:11, (NIV)

Ask God for His Purpose

Have you ever asked God about His plans for your life and your marriage? After all, if God says He has a plan to prosper you, wouldn't you want to know the plan?

A plan refers to a set method, design, or program of action to be followed to accomplish a goal or achieve a desired result. And discovering God's plan for your marriage starts with seeking Him whole-heartedly.

God desires for us to delight in Him. He will help us reach our intended goal when we commit our lives and marriages to Him and trust Him fully.

Don't give up on your marriage just because you have had some difficult times. Set goals and establish godly benchmarks for your marriage, knowing that success in marriage doesn't happen by accident—it requires work and concentrated effort.

After you and your spouse set a goal for your marriage and your family, don't get hung up over the methods used to reach the goals. Men and women do things differently. As a result, our methods for accomplishing the same goal may vary; however, when we remain focused on the goal and lean on God for help, we can accomplish EVERY thing we aspire to achieve.

For example, my husband and I decided we wanted him to be more of a spiritual leader in our home. For me, reading the Bible, listening to ministry resources, and learning about spiritual things came easy. In fact, it's one of my favorite past times, and I love talking about every new thing I learn. Andre is very different. He enjoys reading the Bible and learning scriptures; however, he likes to ponder what he learns. Consequently, it takes him a while to talk about it.

For a long time, I desired for him to share scriptures with our children and lead Bible study with our family; but it seemed as if he was never going to do it—at least not the way I thought he should.

Funny thing, though: whenever I would have one-on-one moments with our children, they would tell me about the lessons their Dad had taught them about God. I learned that he taught them lessons while they were in the car or when he and my son would play basketball together. That's when God helped me realize that Andre was teaching our children and being a spiritual leader in our home—his method was just different from mine; but our goal was the same.

Once, I let go of my view on how it had to be done, I was able to see that it was already being done. God has a plan for your marriage and when you trust Him, you will prosper because in Him, there is hope for your future.

Day thirty

Strategy is easy and execution is really hard…

— John Delaney

A Healthy Marriage Requires a Strategy

Most of us marry for love. We are enticed into believing everything popular songs say about love—Love Will Keep Us Together, All We Need Is Love, I Will Always Love You, Endless Love—and the list goes on. If you're like most people, once you actually get married you quickly realize that love is not all you need. In fact, it's not uncommon after you get married to question everything you ever believed about love.

The truth is marriage requires strategies and tools to last, and love is not a strategy or a tool. A strategy is a plan or a method used to achieve a goal. Tools are the resources used to create, maintain or destroy a thing. Yes, love is required to implement the strategies and use the tools, but love, alone and on its own, will not sustain a marriage.

God, who created marriage, also gave us a strategy for marriage. Those tools and strategies are outlined in Ephesians 5: 21 – 31 and 1 Peter 3:1-9.

Here is the list:

Strategies

- Submit (wives submit to your husbands)
- Sacrifice (husbands sacrifice for your wives)
- Respect (wives respect your husbands)
- Be like-minded
- Be sympathetic
- Do not repay evil with evil

Tools

- The Word of God
- Communication
- Trust
- Forgiveness
- Perseverance
- Faith

If you apply these strategies and tools to your marriage, your marriage will succeed. Finally, remember, God does not create anything to fail; in the end, you win!

We get married expecting marital bliss and looking forward to our happily ever after, however
shortly after the honeymoon, problems,
arguments and frustrations will often occur.
What do you do during the tough times? What
does it all mean for your marriage?

In Think Your Way to a Better Marriage,
Relationship Life Coach, Carnisa Berry encourag-
es you to view your marriage from a perspective
deeper than just your happiness. This 30 day
devotional will transform your thinking and help you have more clarity
and understanding in your marriage.

Marriage can be a wonderful union, but it requires work, healthy thinking and commitment. Think Your Way to a Better Marriage offers strate
gies to assist you with having the marriage of your dreams.

*"Think Your Way to a Better Marriage helped me examine my previous be
haviors in my 14 year marriage. Reflecting on behaviors that didn't produc
any positive results and then using the daily devotional to set the path to c
renewed partnership, resulted in a more intimate and authentic marriage.*
– Meghan K. Branks

"This book is a wonderful resource, it can be such a tool for counseling."
–Tiffany McLeod Bargeman

*"I was truly encouraged while reading Think Your Way to a Better Marriage
What I like most about it is it's not to heavy a read, yet it offers informatio
and points people can be encouraged by and grow from."*
– Cheesette Cowan

ISBN 978-0-616-00291-9

CPSIA information can be obtained
at www.ICGtesting.com
Printed in the USA
BVHW04s0255130818
524223BV00061BA/641/P